EVERYONE WINS!

EVERYONE WINS!

Cooperative Games and Activities

Sambhava and Josette Luvmour
Illustrations by Susan Hill

Published in Cooperation with
Center for Educational Guidance

NEW SOCIETY PUBLISHERS

Cover photo, "Giant Sandals," by Tom Coster. Left to right: Shannon Garrity, Talon Weistar, and Kale Beckwitt.
Book design by Steve Beckwitt.
Illustrations by Susan Hill.

Printed in the U.S.A. by Capital City Press, Montpelier, Vermont.

Inquiries regarding requests to reprint all or part of *Everyone Wins!* should be addressed to New Society Publishers at the address below.

Paperback U.S.A. ISBN: 0-86571-190-9
Paperback Canada ISBN: 1-55092-011-1
Hardback U.S.A. ISBN: 0-86571-189-5
Hardback Canada ISBN: 1-55092-010-3

To order directly from the publishers, please add $3.00 to the price of the first copy, and $1.00 for each additional copy (plus GST in Canada). Send check or money order to:

New Society Publishers,
P.O. Box 189, Gabriola Island, BC V0R 1X0, Canada.

New Society Publishers aims to publish books for fundamental social change through nonviolent action. We focus especially on sustainable living, progressive leadership, and educational and parenting resources. Our full list of books can be browsed on the world wide web at: http://www.swifty.com/nsp/

® ⬭GCU⬭ 745-C

NEW SOCIETY PUBLISHERS
Gabriola Island, BC, Canada and Stony Creek, CT, U.S.A.

About the Authors

In order to practice and promote their work in developmental psychology, Sambhava and Josette Luvmour founded the Center for Educational Guidance (CEG) in 1984. Through CEG, they have led numerous workshops in both Creating Cooperative Learning Environments, and Natural Learning Rhythms, their innovatiove approach to human development. *Mothering, Home Education Magazine, The Community Endeavor* and *New World Times* have published their work. They edit a bimonthly newsletter, *Insight*. With their 14 year old daughter Amber, they homestead 10 acres and run a meditation retreat in North San Juan, CA.

Acknowledgements

"Gratitude is Heaven Itself"

—William Blake

In this spirit we would like to thank the Morgan Family, the Beckwitt Family, the Custer–Weisheimer Family, the Cech Family, Nick Herzmark, and the many folks who have contributed to—

Center for Educational Guidance
Please Treat The Copyright In The Spirit Of Cooperation

The following games are from *The New Games Book* and *More New Games*, ed. Andrew Flugelman, and reprinted with permission from Doubleday, NY, NY.

Dho Dho Dho
Catch the Dragon's Tail
Go Tag
Snake In the Grass
Snow Blind
A What?
Dragon Dodge Ball

The following games are reprinted from *Sharing Nature With Children*, by Joseph Bharat Cornell, Dawn Publications, 14618 Tyler Foote Road, Nevada City, CA 95959.

Blind Trail
Unnature Trail
Duplicate
Tree Silhouettes
Nature Web

Dedication

to Amber

**for the Spirit
in which
she comes to play**

Center for Educational Guidance
offers—
Cooperative Games Workshops

Cooperative Games are tools to be used with skill and sensitivity. **The Cooperative Games Workshop** teaches you to use these tools effectively and successfully. Work with qualified professionals, learning the games and their specific applications.

- Prevent rivalry and violence in the home, classroom and playground.
- Bring together groups of children that have never met.
- Build a child's self esteem.
- Communicate with children effectively.
- Foster friendships that cross social barriers.
- Help children appreciate the wonders and intricacies of Nature.

Your questions from *in life* situations will be answered.

Contact:

Center for Educational Guidance
P.O. Box 445
North San Juan CA 95960
(916)292-3623

Table of Contents

Activity Level Three

Activity Level Four

Activity Level Five

Bibliography

Indices

Introduction

There was big trouble on the playground at the local Waldorf School. Violence was present almost every day and most of the first and second grade children had formed cliques. The parent who had the responsibility for monitoring the playground was getting angrier and angrier and lacked support for coping with the situation. The teachers acknowledged the problem, and saw it as an extension of difficulties in the classroom, but their every attempt to help backfired. The parents blamed other parents and other children for the problem, and the administration and other teachers were growing increasingly alarmed. It was at this point that we were called in. Was there any way to relieve the pressure short of major surgery?

Since this is an introduction to Cooperative Games and Activities we won't describe in detail the different means used to ease the tensions at this school. Cooperative Games and Activities weren't sufficient unto themselves, but they were the critical factor. They not only provided a common ground for all to meet upon but allowed us to test the effectiveness of the other conflict resolution techniques being employed. The games served both diagnostic and remedial purposes.

The first time we met the class on the playground we had them play **Spaghetti**. This was our way saying to them that we are all interconnected and, though sometimes relationships become "knotted up," it is possible to find a solution. **Spaghetti** is played by having everyone stand in a circle, then each person taking the hand of someone not directly next to them. Each person must be holding the hand of two different people. The object is to recreate the circle while continuing to hold hands. This is not easy to do, and there is often no way to do it, but communication and patience are emphasized if there is to be any chance at all. Once children get the idea they want very much to have success. This class played twice, with manners no one would have believed possible, before finally "winning."

Next we played **Rolling Along**. In this game children pair off, lie on their backs and have to roll down a field with their toes connected. At first we let them pick their own partners, then we chose partners randomly and finally we deliberately matched certain students together. Of course there was dissatisfaction with both the random and deliberate methods of pairing, but the game was so much fun, and the release of energy so significant, that the children cooperated.

Next it was into group games such as **Chase in the Ocean** and **True or False**. Then we collectively made an obstacle course, and collectively navigated it. Finally, we played **Hug a Tree**. This was an important moment in the day for this game requires a high degree of trust. Children are in pairs and one is blindfolded. Then, in a fairly dense wood, the sighted child leads the blindfolded partner to a tree by a circuitous route. The blindfolded child explores the tree with all senses but sight. Then, via a different route, the child is led back to start, the blindfold removed and the child has to find the tree.

But how to arrange the pairs? If we put children together who had been having difficulty with one another and they violated trust, it was altogether likely that Cooperative Games would not be energized to healing intensity. If, on the other hand, we allowed the "best friends" who formed the core of the cliques to pair off, then there was the probability that those cliques would be reinforced.

The understanding of how the students were connected had been developing in us during the time the previous games were being played. We relied on no other persons judgment, not even that of the teacher. It is in the course of the games, while involvement is total, that the child will forget the more superficial aspects of image and react according to needs. For instance, two boys who were often the object of one another's aggression had greatly enjoyed being paired in **Rolling Along**. They moved across the field so quickly that the other children were delighted and stopped to watch them. Everyone was surprised, and a comfortable, when they realized the new roles these boys were living.

In every group there are those who have the capability of providing a "neutralizing" influence. Often this capability is hidden, for there is great pressure to join one side or another. In this class of first and second graders the neutralizers were well underground. Communication and "safe space" had deteriorated to that extent. But we had spotted them during the group games. They played the games for the enjoyment of it, and did not worry who was next to them. They looked to us for information as to how best to play and were not afraid of telling those who interfered to be quiet.

The biggest clue to the identity of the neutralizers was their need to let us know they were not identified with any one group of children. They let us know in subtle and not so subtle ways. One child would deliberately stand apart from the group while awaiting the next round of play. Another would deliberately join in with a child or group she didn't usually join, and would give us a verbal sign that she was doing so.

The neutralizers played a critical role in the games which followed. We split the more closely attached of the cliques among them. The rest we arranged so that they were with children they weren't ordinarily with, or ones with whom they had moderate difficulties. It worked out very well. By now our allotted time was spent and it was with a groan of displeasure that the children returned to the classroom.

Over the next few weeks the parent who was in charge of the playground was trained. Gradually, more and more complex games were introduced, each time expanding the children's perception of safe space. Eventually we played games like **Cast Your Vote** and **Interview** in which they could express their understanding of, and desires for, their classroom. To do so took great courage on their part, and it was not readily forthcoming. There were other difficulties in the relationship of the classroom teacher and the parents, but finally the class reached a place where, at least in the playground, they could channel their energy into cooperation.

Principles of Application

Cooperative Games are a tool, and like all tools they must be used with skill and sensitivity. One of the beautiful and exciting aspects of Cooperative Games and Activities is that they can be varied according to the ages and talents of the participants; they can be adapted to every learning situation. Vary the games to fit the profile of the participants.

Age is a factor for each game. Please do not take age guidelines literally; experiment, and enjoy as you go along. But it is important to consider age, and at a deeper level, the growth stage of the children.

A thorough and meaningful understanding of the growth stages of children is one the best tools for all education. Success with these games depends in large measure on your understanding of child development. With this understanding, games can be chosen and applied with an efficacy that is astounding.

The attitude of the game leader is critical. Children are naturally attuned to accept guidance from elders and so are able to read us in disarmingly straightforward ways. If the leader does not genuinely wish for cooperation, or in any way exhibits prejudice or manipulation, the playing of Cooperative Games becomes hypocritical. **As you model, so you teach.**

If a game does not work well the first time, come back to it later. Sometimes it takes several attempts before children grasp the sense of the games. Cooperative Games and Activities are not woven into the fabric of American play. Children have not been watching the games on TV since they were born. Therefore, go slowly. Do not attempt too many variations immediately. That creates the image of desperation. It is better to try lots of different games. Be honest, be patient and enlist the children's help.

If a child does not want to play, do not force her. Do not allow her to disrupt the group either. Our experience has been that after observing, most children join, or find a different constructive activity. There is something about the cooperative nature of the event that increases a child's safe space. The atmosphere becomes gentler and the children sense it.

Go ahead and play. Read through the games once or twice, familiarize yourself with ones you are to play that day, and then go for it. Why not? You've got nothing to lose. Your ability to facilitate will come from experience and will come rather quickly.

Bring your sense of humor. This is the most important point of all. Make jokes, even bad ones. Lighten up, play games and let everyone enjoy themselves. Humor is the most healthy environment for everyone, and one in which you will have access to the most information concerning the children.

Games in Different Situations

Cooperative Games and Activities have been used successfully in all learning environments, at parties, within the immediate family and the extended family, and at large group gatherings. We have played them with whole communities, camps, public and private schools, the disabled, and home schooling collectives. They provide an excellent focus that allows appreciation of everyone's abilities in a friendly comfortable way. Self esteem grows; the inner sense of peace and interconnectedness comes alive.

There are games that serve as ice-breakers, as a medium for feelings, as concentration intensifiers, as artistic and thinking enhancers, and as group and individual centering techniques. With a minimum of effort and maximum of fun, Cooperative Games provide a way to recognize and integrate the rhythms of the participants.

In the experience described at the beginning of this article the situation was conflict within a large school group. We would like to close with descriptions of two more experiences, each of a very different nature. These three examples hardly exhaust all the situations amenable to the use of Cooperative Games. Hopefully, taken together, they will stimulate you to finding your own approach to using them. If more information is required, feel free to write to us. We are sure we can create an application suitable for your situation.

We have the honor of guiding a group of children on a nature walk every Friday. There are about a dozen in the class, ranging in age from 6 to 12. Our rhythm is to take an hour walk in the forest that surrounds our community, have a snack and then play cooperative games. We have lunch and then it is more games, or story telling, or acting. The aim of the class is for the children to learn how to be friends. This aim they know. When conflict arises we stop our activity and work towards resolution. No cliques are allowed. We all agree that being friends is not that easy. Every one of them is glad for the opportunity to learn. They are also angry that this skill is not usually taught for they clearly perceive the trouble grown-ups have relating.

Surprisingly, nature is not the primary attraction for the children. That honor belongs to Cooperative Games and Activities and the social dynamic arising therefrom. When we come across the red tail hawk doing a mating flight, or examine coyote scat to determine its diet, or surprise a flock of wild turkeys, or collect wild flowers to press, there is always great delight, wonder and appreciation of nature. But these are not sought. The children would rather play cooperative games. This, to us, is something of a shock, but a tribute to the power of these games in satisfying a genuine need of the children.

Their favorite game will not be found listed in this book. They created it themselves and, to be honest, we do not know all the rules. We're not sure that anyone does. It is called "Wild Horses" and it has something to do with play acting horses, mountain lions, Indians, "White Men", sheep, Medicine Women, and whatever or whomever any participant wants to be. This game has evolved from a game they invented about the Greek Myths. All we ask is that everyone be included, that there be no real violence, and that no cliques form. At first there was some resistance to these guidelines, but now they need not even be mentioned. Every now and then we check in with different children to make sure they are included in a satisfactory way. We've yet to be disappointed.

"Wild Horses" did not appear until the class had been together over a year. We had gone through many games, most of them with success. Most games had their moment of being preferred, but, on the whole, each has had a similar amount of consideration. Often the children came up with their own variations.

One last experience concerns a mother and her six year old boy. We were asked to help when the mother was just concluding a painful and violent divorce from the father. The boy — bright, energetic and sensitive — was having a difficult time in school. He is strong and likes the spotlight. His classmates had seized upon this to use him to personify their own negative tendencies. As a result he was often dared and taunted. Like his father, he responded violently. The label of "bad" was hung on him and any time the others needed to participate in "badness", this boy was the chosen object.

And, to be sure, part of him liked it. It was attention and power and even those who did not like him, needed him. One boy, frail in body and underdeveloped emotionally, particularly enjoyed leaning on him, getting hit, and both of them being punished.

While work with this family proceeded on many levels, one small but important part involved cooperative games. We wanted to reawaken the boy's sense of belongingness. If he could feel that he belonged on this planet and in his family then his life would be of value and destructive behaviors would diminish.

Two cooperative games were chosen and both worked very well. First, to give the mother the information of the disposition of the boy each day, an animal game was introduced around the breakfast table. The mother had many pictures of animals. Each morning she would hold one up and each person would say how they resembled that animal that day. She had everything from rearing cobras to cuddling koalas. There was a younger sister in the house and the three of them would play together. Often they acted out their animal feelings. Of course, their moods became family knowledge and that instantly released some tension. And the mother had a much clearer picture of how to apply other remedies we were using in our attempt to improve the overall situation.

The other game was a morning family stretch game. Like the one above, it is very simple. Everyone meets by the fire for a five minute stretch together, with each family member being the leader on a rotating basis. They soon added the variation of a hand coordination game. They now started their day taking a relaxed breath together. The connection that the boy needed to experience was present. He responded favorably and his good health was soon restored.

Friends, thank you for giving us the opportunity to write about Cooperative Games and Activities. We truly hope you will experiment with them and find them as useful as we have. In this critical juncture of human evolution they can help teach cooperation, respect, and friendship. These are qualities that go a long way, and of which we can never get enough.

If we can be of any help to you, do not hesitate to write.

Peace,

Josette Luvmour, Director
Sambhava Luvmour, Director
Center for Educational Guidance
P.O. Box 445
North San Juan CA 95960-0445
(916)292-3623

Center for Educational Guidance
is a non-profit corporation.

How To Use This Book

Under the name of each game you will find four categories containing information to help you evaluate its usefulness in different situations. These categories are:

Activity Level—"1" is the most active and "5" is the least active. The games are arranged by Activity Level. You will find the "1's" first, then "2's", "3's", "4's" and finally "5's".

Age—refers to the minimum age a participant needs to be to enjoy the game. All games are *indexed* as to Age in the back of the book.

Location—"In" means that the game is best played Indoors. "Out" means it must be played outdoors. "In/Out" means the game can be played indoors or outdoors.

Group Size—refers to the minimum amount of players necessary to play the game. All games are *indexed* as to Group Size in the back of the book.

How to Use the Indexes

Games within an index are in alphabetical order. Thus if you want to find a game that needs six players, go to the Group Size index and look up "Six or More." The games are alphabetically listed. If your players are seven and eight years old, then go to the Age index, look up the age and cross reference with those games selected from the Group Size index. You are now ready to play.

The body of the game information consists of the **Description**, **Variations** and **Hints**. If **Materials** are needed they are indicated in this section as well. Don't be afraid to try your own **Variations**. And please drop us a line with any new **Hints** you might uncover in your play.

Catch the Dragon's Tail *(page 11) — note the hankerchief in the rear pocket of the "tail."*

Dragon Dodge Ball *(page 12) — increase the excitement by adding more balls and speeding the pace.*

Chase In the Ocean

Activity Level: 1   Age Level: 4+
Location: In or Outside   Group Size: 6

Game Description:

A caller shouts "ship" and all the children run to the base at which she points. After counting three, the caller chases with arms outspread ready to gobble any child not on the base and touching another. The caller—if older—usually just misses.

Variations:

Sardine—all the children must be on base and touching one another. *Crab*—the children must be back to back with one another.

Special Hints:

Make three or four areas to run to so caller can surprise the children by pointing as she calls.

Smaug's Jewels

Activity Level: 1   Age Level: 4+
Location: In or Outside   Group Size: 5
Materials: a rag

Game Description:

The "treasure"—a rag—is placed on the ground. One child guards it. All the others try to grab it. If a thief is touched by the guardian of the treasure she takes three steps back.

Variations:

Play with two guardians and allow free players to un-freeze frozen players by tagging.

Special Hints:

Be the referee.

1

Dho - Dho - Dho

Activity Level: 1   Age Level: 7+

Location: In or Outside   Group Size: 8

Game Description:

Two teams face off. While holding her breath, one player from a team crosses the line and tries to tag one or more players and make it back to her side all the time holding her breath and with enough air left to say Dho-Dho-Dho. All tagged players switch teams. If the player does not succeed she joins the other team.

Variations:

Vary playing area size.

Special Hints:

Not fully cooperative so monitor closely. Valuable for energetic ones to let off steam.

Big Toe

Activity Level: 1   Age Level: 7+

Location: In or Outside   Group Size: 1

Game Description:

Squat down, grab your toes, bend your knees and try to jump forward as far as possible.

Variations:

Do it as a collective long jump or choreograph as a dance.

Special Hints:

You'll improve with practice. It is funny as a group.

On Your Knees

Activity Level: 1

Age Level: 7+

Location: In or Outside

Group Size: 1

Game Description:
Kneel down with back straight, lift heels towards rump and grab ankles. Take knee steps as you are now balanced on your kneecaps.

Variations:
Try it as a group—grabbing a partner's ankle in a relay race or a dance.

Special Hints:
Make sure no knees get hurt.

Hop As One

Activity Level: 1

Age Level: 5+

Location: In or Outside

Group Size: 5

Game Description:
Players in a line—except for the leader—lift and extend left leg so the person behind can grab ankle or heel. They then place right hand on right shoulder of person in front for support. Now it is hop time.

Variations:
Switch sides — do a dance — collective timing — over obstacles.

Special Hints:
Remind them of careful coordination. Practice before getting discouraged.

Upside Down Cycling

Activity Level: 1   Age Level: 4+

Location: In or Outside Group Size: 2

Game Description:

Lie on back and touch bottom of feet with bottom of partners feet. Do simultaneous cycling action first in one direction then in another.

Variations:

Try three, eyes closed, use music.

Special Hints:

Works well for all shapes and sizes of people — even those in conflict.

Emotional Relay Race

Activity Level: 1   Age Level: 9+

Location: In or Outside Group Size: 12

Materials: Three bowls and three pieces of fruit.

Game Description:

Three teams—each lined up behind the piece of fruit of its choice. Each player takes time to come up with their sound and movement for "*sad*", "*angry*" and "*happy*". The bowls are a set distance away. Each player picks up the fruit—runs to the bowl—puts it down—does "*angry*" three times—runs back to start—does "*happy*" twice— back to fruit for "*sad*" twice—brings the fruit back to start—takes a bite—and the next player goes.

Variations:

Can substitute other emotions or do it in tandem.

Special Hints:

Nine and older. Players should be in playful mood right from the start.

Giants - Wizards - Elves

Activity Level: 1

Age Level: 5+

Location: In or Outside

Group Size: 8

Game Description:

Two teams. Each team agrees on a posture for a giant, a wizard and an elf and shows it to the other team. Each huddles and decides which creature it will be. Teams come to center line and at the count of three make the chosen posture and say the creatures name. Wizards fool Giants—Giants beat Elves—Elves trick Wizards. Whoever loses has to beat it back to their safety about 20 feet away from center line before the other team catches them. Those caught switch teams.

Special Hints:

Similar to Rock–Paper–Scissors with action

Blow the Ball

Activity Level: 1

Age Level: 4+

Location: Inside

Group Size: 5

Materials: Ping pong ball, mats or blankets

Game Description:

One child lies on stomach on a mat. Six others grab edges of the mat and pull while the child blows the ping pong ball across the room. How fast can they do it?

Variations:

As a relay race with or without obstacles

Special Hints:

Make sure no one player is over burdened

Hug Tag

Activity Level: 1   Age Level: 4+
Location: Outside   Group Size: 8
Materials: strips of cloth, hats or easily held objects

Game Description:

About ⅙ of the group are given a strip of cloth. They are "**it**" and can tag any other player. The others are safe only when hugging another player. If two or more players keep hugging, "**it**" can take three steps backwards and say "**1,2,3 Break!**" Those players have to find new players to hug.

Special Hints:

Pick boundaries carefully. Keep the game moving. Great fun for everyone. Equalizes varied talents.

Up and Around

Activity Level: 1   Age Level: 8+
Location: Outside   Group Size: 2
Materials: two foot stick, belts, string, rubber ball

Game Description:

With a string, tied to a broomstick, hang a tennis ball just above the ground. Children support the stick at their waists against their belts. Without using their hands they try to swing the ball over the stick.

Variations:

Make it wind and unwind. Play with eyes closed.

Special Hints:

Let little ones use hands.

Cooperative Relay Races

Activity Level: 1   Age Level: 5+
Location: Outside   Group Size: 8+
Materials: Varies according to type of race.

Game Description:

Divide children into teams. They race for a best collective time while negotiating a course.

Variations:

Obstacles—crawling—run backwards—skipping—with golf ball in spoon.

Special Hints:

Let children make up their own order of running; be prepared to be crazy.

Creative Monkey Bars

Activity Level: 1   Age Level: 6+
Location: Outside   Group Size: 3
Materials: PVC pipe and fittings

Game Description:

Using PVC pipe and fittings, children design and construct and play on their own monkey bars.

Variations:

Make their own furniture

Special Hints:

Materials can be expensive, but self esteem is worth it!

Obstacle Course

Activity Level: 1

Age Level: 3+

Location: Outside

Group Size: 5

Materials: Anything and everything

Game Description:

Children design their own obstacle course and run it.

Variations:

Infinite

Special Hints:

Make sure all who want to participate have a chance to do so.

Pull Together

Activity Level: 1

Age Level: 5+

Location: Outside

Group Size: 10

Materials: Large strong rope.

Game Description:

Elder divides children into two equal teams so when they pull on the rope as hard as they can, neither team moves.

Variations:

Tie a rope around a heavy object and try to move it.

Special Hints:

Switch children so that balance is achieved. When they get the idea encourage them to switch themselves.

Blanket Volley Ball

Activity Level: 1
Location: Outside
Materials: Blankets, balls.

Age Level: 8+
Group Size: 6

Game Description:

Players hold the edge of the blanket. They place a ball on the blanket. They then toss the ball up by cooperatively manipulating the blanket. They they try to catch it in the middle of the blanket. Score is cumulative.

Variations:

Use volley ball, beach ball. Change blanket size, define boundaries, use net. Pass ball between two groups with blankets.

Special Hints:

Switch positions on blanket—make sure little ones do not get hurt. Skill needed. Greatly helps energetic ones to center in cooperation.

Couples Sports

Activity Level: 1
Location: Outside
Materials: Balls, leg ties

Age Level: 8+
Group Size: 10

Game Description:

Play baseball with legs tied together or holding hands.

Variations:

Any ball game or tag

Special Hints:

Match pairs with attention to athletic ability. Use small playing space.

True or False

Activity Level: 1   Age Level: 7+
Location: Outside   Group Size: 8

Game Description:

Two teams, *Trues* or *Falses*, face off in the middle of a field with a safety area for each team about 20 feet behind. Elder makes a statement about nature. If correct *Trues* chase *Falses*. If incorrect *Falses* chase *Trues*. Anyone caught goes to the other team.

Variations:

Statements about academics, or any other subject.

Special Hints:

Let confusion reign before supplying the correct answer. Choose questions appropriate to knowledge of player. This is an excellent teaching game

How Do You Do?

Activity Level: 1   Age Level: 8+
Location: Outside   Group Size: 10

Game Description:

All but two players join hands in a circle. The outside two are a lost ship looking for port. They choose a pair from the circle. Holding hands, the chosen pair and the outside pair run around the circle in opposite directions attempting to get back to the vacant spot. As they pass one another, they must stop, shake hands, say "How Do You Do?" before continuing.

Variations:

Hop or skip around the circle. Do with eyes closed and runners touching the circle as they move.

Special Hints:

Explain rules and direction of travel carefully. Warn against crashes. Make sure all get a turn.

Catch the Dragon's Tail

Activity Level: 1   Age Level: 7+

Location: Outside   Group Size: 8

Materials: Handkerchief

Game Description:

Players line up with arms around the waist of the person in front. Last one has a handkerchief in her pocket. The player at the head of the line tries to grab the handkerchief. No part of Dragon may break.

Variations:

Two Dragons attempt to catch each other's tails. Rotate the players.

It

Activity Level: 1   Age Level: 6+

Location: Outside   Group Size: 16

Game Description:

Two teams. Each goes to a different tree, leaving about 150 feet between them. One player calls **It** and starts running toward the other tree. If she touches the tree she scores a point. But anyone who touches her or is touched by her automatically is **It**. She can deliberately touch another on her team, who then continues towards the same goal. But if touched by a member of the other team, **It** is transferred and that player tries to move to her tree. No one can block or help the runner as she advances towards her tree.

Special Hints:

It is as if a spirit is being transferred at touch. Points are hard to score but not impossible.

Toby Terrific Turtle

Activity Level: 1   Age Level: 6+
Location: Outside   Group Size: 5
Materials: Obstacles, green clothes, old blanket

Game Description:

Group huddles under blanket. All are blindfolded except the leader. Group moves together through obstacles as quickly as possible. Everyone gets a chance to be leader.

Variations:

Play in mud puddles! Group can hold hands.

Special Hints:

Be careful!

Dragon Dodge Ball

Activity Level: 1   Age Level: 5+
Location: Outside   Group Size: 7+
Materials: Sponge balls or rubber balls.

Game Description:

All join hands in a large circle. Two people form a dragon. One, the head, stands upright, the other, the tail, holds the head's hips and sticks her fanny out. The others pass ball around and try to hit the Dragon's fanny. If a ball hits the ground it must be passed before being thrown at the Dragon. No player can hold a ball more than three seconds. Passer who sets up the hit becomes the new tail. The former tail becomes the head. Use at least two balls at a time.

Variations:

More dragons—vary circle size.

Special Hints:

Warn against collisions. Excellent for working out aggression.

Go Tag *(page 13) — note players lined up facing in alternate directions.*

Rope Raising *(page 17) — for fun try to repeat the raising and sitting with a coordinated rhythm.*

Go Tag

Activity Level: 1   Age Level: 8+
Location: Outside   Group Size: 10

Game Description:

Everyone squats in a line—alternate players facing opposite directions,to the right and left. Everyone but person in front—*the chaser*—or back—*the chased*—kneels. The *chaser* can tap a squatter who then takes up the chase. The first *chaser* takes the squatter's position. The chaser must always go in the same direction. The chased can go either direction. For example: players **1** through **10** line up. **1-3-5-7-9** face to the right. **2-4-6-8-10** face to the left. **1** chases **10**. **1** decides **7** has a better chance to tag **10**, so **1** taps **7** and takes her place. **7** picks up the chase. It's a game of timing and cunning.

Special Hints:

Practice a few times so all understand. Give everyone a chance to do everything.

Come Together

Activity Level: 2   Age Level: 5+
Location: In or Outside   Group Size: 2

Game Description:

Two players stand at opposite ends of a room then run toward one another and leap. The object is to land as close as possible without touching one another.

Variations:

Land side by side—shake hands while passing in the air—turn around in the air and land close together.

Special Hints:

Needs several practice attempts before it becomes a game. Be careful.

Wheelbarrow

Activity Level: 2   Age Level: 6+

Location: In or Outside   Group Size: 2+

Game Description:

In pairs one child holds both legs of the other while that child moves on her hands.

Variations:

Choreograph movements—the movements of several pairs—introduce obstacles—blindfolds etc.

Special Hints:

Make sure each goes at their own speed—switch partners

Octopus

Activity Level: 2   Age Level: 4+

Location: In or Outside   Group Size: 5

Game Description:

In a defined area one child is the *Octopus*. He attempts to tag another. When he does that child is frozen but can wave its arms like the tentacles of an *octopus* helping tag others until all are *octopi*.

Variations:

All the tag variations. Vary play area's size and location.

Special Hints:

Use big boundaries.

Lemonade

Activity Level: 2   Age Level: 4+
Location: In or Outside   Group Size: 8

Game Description:

Two teams each with a safety area about 20 feet behind face off in the middle. One team has decided on the role (e.g. astronauts, clowns, scuba divers, etc.) they are going to pantomime. The other team guesses. When someone guesses right the pantomimists race for their safety area. The other team chases. Anyone tagged switches teams.

Variations:

Include scenes from nature, literature or fantasy roles, e.g. being clouds.

Special Hints:

Help the little ones. Everyone loves this game. It brings groups together.

Dolphin and Fish

Activity Level: 2   Age Level: 5+
Location: In or Outside   Group Size: 8

Game Description:

All but two players circle and hold hands. One free player is a *dolphin* and the other is a *fish*. *Dolphin* chases *fish*. When *fish* runs through the circle children raise their arms; but when *dolphin* tries to get through they lower them.

Special Hints:

No favoritism among the children. Help the slow by altering the rules

Popcorn Balls

Activity Level: 2   Age Level: 3+
Location: In or Outside   Group Size: 7

Game Description:

Children crouch on the floor. Everyone chants: —Popcorn Balls, Popcorn Balls, Popcorn Balls—sounding like a locomotive. Adult tells the children that as the floor—*the pan*—heats up; the children—*the popcorn*—start hopping—*popping*—all over the place. When two children bump each other while *popping*, they stick together. The game is over when all are one ball.

Special Hints:

Good for the little ones.

Standing Together

Activity Level: 2   Age Level: 8+
Location: In or Outside   Group Size: 4

Game Description:

Seated in a circle players grasp arms or hands and try to collectively stand up.

Variations:

Larger groups—grabbing people not next to one another.

Special Hints:

Let the group experiment—go slowly—the more people the harder it is.

16

Rope Raising

Activity Level: 2   Age Level: 8+

Location: In or Outside   Group Size: 10

Materials: Large rope tied at its ends to form a circle

Game Description:

Seated in a circle group all pull on the rope with their hands so that they stand at once.

Variations:

Stretch rope out in a line and make two equal teams at ends, pull together so that everyone stands up.

Special Hints:

Coach the children to pull together; watch out for the energetic kids criticizing the less active ones.

Rolling Along

Activity Level: 2   Age Level: 3+

Location: In or Outside   Group Size: 2

Game Description:

In pairs, partners lie stretched out on floor, toe-to-toe, heads in opposite direction; they attempt to roll across the floor keeping toes connected.

Variations:

Only toes of one foot connected, while sitting in an "L" position.

Special Hints:

Keep sending one pair down after the next—use verbal encouragement. Make pairs carefully.

Hawk & Mouse

Activity Level: 2   Age Level: 6+
Location: In or Outside   Group Size: 6

Game Description:

Two blindfolded children are in the middle of the circle. One is a local predator, the other is its prey. The rest of the children keep them safely in the circle. The predator tries to find the prey who has a little bell around neck. No talking.

Variations:

Anytime predator makes its sound, prey must answer.

Special Hints:

Make the circle smaller if the predator has trouble finding the prey; remind children not to let anyone fall.

Amigos All

Activity Level: 2   Age Level: 5+
Location: In or Outside   Group Size: 7
Materials: Bean bags

Game Description:

Children walk at their own pace balancing a bean bag on their head. Leader controls the pace. If bean bag falls the child is frozen. Another child must pick up the bean bag and place it on that child's head without losing her own.

Variations:

Many movements—over obstacles—cooperative relay race—to music—give the kids opportunity to lead and come up with their own variations.

Special Hints:

If too difficult let little ones use one hand.

18

Beam Walk

Activity Level: 2

Location: In or Outside

Age Level: 5+

Group Size: 1

Game Description:

Children practice on balance beams, such as on supported 4x4's—many cooperative possibilities to try.

Variations:

Music, obstacles, pairs, etc.

Special Hints:

Be Safe! Builds self esteem if approached gently.

Snake in the Grass

Activity Level: 2

Location: In or Outside

Age Level: 5+

Group Size: 5

Game Description:

One player is the *snake* in the grass and lies and slithers around on her belly. All other players touch one part of the *snake's* body. When ready, trying to surprise, she says **"Snake in the Grass"** and tries to tag players. Anyone tagged becomes a *snake* until all are tagged.

Variations:

Change boundaries—allow *snakes* to be *alligators* or *bears*(move on hands and knees).

Special Hints:

Shoes off if possible, keep the players challenging the *snake*.

Up and Over

Activity Level: 2

Age Level: 5+

Location: In or Outside

Group Size: 10

Materials: Anything that happens to be around.

Game Description:

Divide the children into small groups of various sizes. Each group makes itself into a human obstacle. Players then have to run the course. When they get to an obstacle the obstacle tells them how to get past it. As players pass an obstacle, they join the end of the line to traverse remaining obstacles. As group finishes the course it makes a new obstacle while all other players are still on previous obstacles. It can go on this way for hours.

Variations:

Add non-human obstacles—allow no talking—increase number of people comprising each obstacle. Add skills such as dribbling a ball while running the course.

Special Hints:

Watch carefully and learn about your players; much is revealed in this activity.

One Big Slug

Activity Level: 2

Age Level: 4+

Location: In or Outside

Group Size: 4

Materials: Mats, things for an obstacle course

Game Description:

Children build an obstacle course. Then they connect into groups of four and, while holding the ankles of the one in front, go through the course on hands and knees.

Variations:

Cover all their bodies but heads with a blanket.

Snowblind

Activity Level: 2

Age Level: 5+

Location: In or Outside

Group Size: 5

Materials: A long foam sword or suitable padded substitute

Game Description:

"It" is blindfolded has the sword and chants for 10 seconds. Rest of players run inside the boundaries and assume a stationary crouch when chant stops. "It" moves around trying to tag players with sword.

Variations:

Players stay still after chant stops. Anyone tagged joins "It" and next round begins with the "Its" chanting and players moving.

Special Hints:

Make sure sword is soft and modify boundaries according to abilities of players.

All of Us, All At Once

Activity Level: 2

Age Level: 1+

Location: In or Outside

Group Size: 2

Materials: Anything and everything

Game Description:

Leader suggests things to be and the group "is" them collectively.

Variations:

As varied as your imagination.

Special Hints:

Perfect for integrating new people and different ages.

Dances of the Mind

Activity Level: 2   Age Level: 3+
Location: In or Outside   Group Size: 3+

Game Description:

Have the children form a dance as an expression of a chosen concept i.e. high–low and medium

Variations:

colors—time—relatives, aggressions etc. Use music as appropriate. Let the older ones pick their own.

Special Hints:

Help them along. Filter sarcasm. Once in progress a great builder of self esteem and non verbal communication skills.

See Saw

Activity Level: 2   Age Level: 8+
Location: In or Outside   Group Size: 2

Game Description:

Facing one another partners sit with knees bent up and bottoms of their feet on the floor. They slip their feet just under the cheeks of the other's behind—join hands—and move by back and forward rocking motion.

Variations:

Reverse directions—make it coop relay race—use obstacles.

Special Hints:

End by coming to a standing position.

Cooperative Juggle

Activity Level: 2

Location: In or Outside

Materials: Balls

Age Level: 8+

Group Size: 5

Game Description:

Player 1 throws ball to any other player. The receiver says her name as she catches it. She then throws to another, who after saying her name, throws to another until all have had one chance. As the ball goes around a second time, the thrower says the name of the person to whom she is throwing. Players throw to same person each time. Keep adding balls to see how many can be juggled. Each time a ball is thrown, the thrower must call the name of the receiver. Player 1 initiates each ball.

Variations:

Large groups or small. Use yarn, socks, or anything soft instead of ball. *Connecting Eyes* is group juggling with many objects being thrown to anyone; all the thrower has to do is establish eye contact with the receiver.

Special Hints:

Good icebreaker—lots of fun. Let those having conflict play by themselves with many balls.

Don't Use Your Teeth

Activity Level: 2

Age Level: 6+

Location: Outside

Group Size: 3

Materials: Tube sock or old towel

Game Description:

One player stands a short distance from the other two and throws a knotted sock or towel towards them. They have to catch it with their bodies but without using their hands.

Variations:

Back to back. One of the two catchers closes eyes.

Special Hints:

A good way to let active children who are having trouble being together work it out.

Shape Tag

Activity Level: 2

Age Level: 6+

Location: Outside

Group Size: 5

Game Description:

Three players form a triangle. A fourth is "it" and a fifth tries to avoid being tagged. The triangle protects the fifth by changing shapes. Make play area boundaries with no tagging across the triangle.

Variations:

People making triangle keep hands on each other's shoulders. Try multiple triangles with equal number of chasers and chased. Let any chaser catch anyone being chased.

Special Hints:

Change boundaries so no one is "it" for too long. Triangle Tag can slip into competitiveness so be careful.

Base Ball Pass

Activity Level: 2   Age Level: 7+
Location: Outside   Group Size: 8
Materials: Large balls

Game Description:

Four players and one large ball start at each of four
bases. Two players move their ball to the next base
without using hands and pass the ball to the waiting
pair. They then await the next pair coming behind them
to pass them another ball which they move to the next
base and pass on.

Variations:

Three on a team—vary amount of bases.

Special Hints:

Keep the game moving—help the slower ones.

Moving Ladder

Activity Level: 2   Age Level: 6+
Location: Outside   Group Size: 6
Materials: sturdy ladder

Game Description:

Players spread out along both sides of the ladder and
lift it so that it is held horizontally at their waist. One
end is lowered and the *traveller* crawls on. The ladder is
raised and the *traveller* crawls the length of the ladder.

Variations:

Use a plank—change the angle of the ladder—walk
the ladder around.

Special Hints:

Watch for tiring ladder holders and for show-offs.

Garden

Activity Level: 2

Age Level: 1+

Location: Outside

Group Size: 1

Materials: Compost, fertilizers, shovels, seeds, soil, water, fencing (if necessary).

Game Description:

Make an organic garden of whatever size is appropriate. Make it as a family, school, group, class, or community effort.

Variations:

Herb gardens—seed gardens—sprout gardens—wild flower gardens

Special Hints:

Grow something year round.

Blind Trail

Activity Level: 2

Age Level: 8+

Location: Outside

Group Size: 6

Materials: Rope/blindfolds

Game Description:

Blindfolded players are guided through a part of the forest by feeling their way along a rope that has been placed there by the elder. The elder removes the rope when players get to end. Players uncover their eyes and find their way back to the beginning place.

Variations:

Across level areas, across a stream, over logs. If players are old enough use a very long rope.

Special Hints:

Emphasize calm awareness—vary complexity.

Cooperative Musical Chairs

Activity Level: 2

Location:In or Out

Age Level: 3+

Group Size: 5

Materials: Music, floor pillows

Game Description:

Just like musical chairs, except that when the music stops and one pillow is removed, the remaining players all have to sit or touch the remaining pillows.

Variations:

Have all players sit on top of one another. Be careful no one gets hurt.

Indian Log Pass

Activity Level: 2

Location: Outside

Age Level: 7+

Group Size: 8

Materials: Big log

Game Description:

Each player gets a number, starting with one. Players line up on a log in order. Now player **one** must switch places with the last player (from other end) without falling off the log. Then player **two** switches places with the next–to–the–last player and so–on till all have switched.

Variations:

Try with various conditions e.g., no talking, switchers blindfolded or one hand on top of head.

Special Hints:

Make instructions clear at the beginning. **Be safe!**

Walking Together

Activity Level: 2

Age Level: 8+

Location: Outside

Group Size: 3

Materials: 2—10 foot long 2" by 4" studs, 12—4" long leather straps or nylon webbing, screws.

Game Description:

Six leather straps—for footholds—are screwed into each stud. Six people slip their feet into the straps—left feet in one "sandal"—right feet in the other "sandal"—and try to walk as a unit.

Variations:

Move over or through obstacles, dance, move sideways. Try indoors with pieces of carpet. Try various lengths of 2 by 4 studs.

Special Hints:

Make sure they practice before trying difficult maneuvers. **Be safe.**

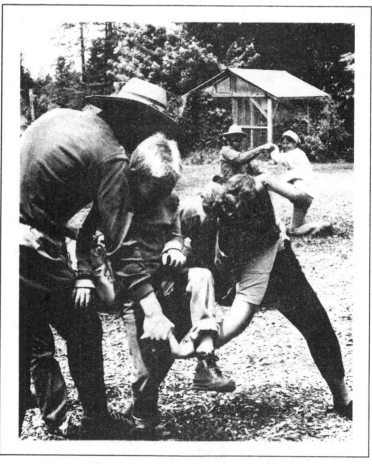

Up and Over *(page 20) — obstacles can help the players through "themselves."*

What Does this Mean?

Activity Level: 3   Age Level: 5+

Location: In or Outside   Group Size: 4

Materials: Anything and everything

Game Description:

Each player is told to find an object that has a special value for her. Discussion follows during which each child tells how the object exemplifies her value. For example—a rock represents friendship because of its solidity or the moon is caring due to lighting the earth at night.

Variations:

Restrict objects to nature. Agree on one value for the entire class and have everyone find different representations of it.

Special Hints:

Give examples—encourage free expression—participate yourself.

29   *Hug A Tree*

Rhythm Sticks

Activity Level: 3	Age Level: 6+
Location: In or Outside	Group Size: 2

Materials: Cut one inch dowels about 18" long, music

Game Description:

Children sit cross-legged facing one another. They establish a rhythm with their sticks by hitting their own sticks together—hitting the floor—hitting each other's sticks. Then do it to music.

Variations:

Vary group size—use one hand only—let the children sing their own music—try it blindfolded.

Special Hints:

Play along and have fun. Vary the ages playing together. Let some children make music with other instruments. Enhances musical and nonverbal communication skills.

Wheel

Activity Level: 3	Age Level: 4+
Location: In or Outside	Group Size: 5

Game Description:

All players stand sideways in a circle and put hands towards the middle. They are now spokes of a wheel. Turn and move around the room.

Variations:

Hopping and or skipping—over obstacles—eyes closed.

Special Hints:

Increase complexity to keep interest high. Best for the very young.

Where Were You?

Activity Level: 3　　　　　Age Level: 5+
Location: In or Outside　　Group Size: 12

Game Description:

Leader stands in the middle. Children are in four teams on her left, right, in front and behind. Children are still while leader turns in a circle and stops. Then teams reposition themselves as they were before—on the left, right, front and back.

Variations:

Collectively time them.

Special Hints:

Best to have 16 or 20 kids.

Stiff As A Board

Activity Level: 3　　　　　Age Level: 5+
Location: In or Outside　　Group Size: 5

Game Description:

One player lies on the ground as stiff as possible. The others pick her up and carry her as far as they can.

Variations:

Make it a relay race—over obstacles—balance a glass of water on the back of the one being carried.

Special Hints:

Make sure no one is straining. No jokes or put-downs about another child's anatomy.

Down the Hole

Activity Level: 3　　　　　Age Level: 5+
Location: In or Outside　　Group Size: 6
Materials: Old sheet or bedspread, ball

Game Description:

Cut a small hole, just big enough for the ball, in the center of the bedspread or sheet. Children hold the edges of the sheet and try to get the ball to go through the hole.

Variations:

Use several balls, try a parachute instead of a sheet.

Special Hints:

Great fun, brings group to a "center."

Down the Tube

Activity Level: 3　　　　　Age Level: 5+
Location: In or Outside　　Group Size: 2
Materials: Ping pong ball, cardboard tube such as from toilet tissue roll.

Game Description:

Toss the ball back and forth trying to catch it in the tube.

Variations:

Use a ring instead of ping pong ball and try to catch it on a stick. Vary distance between players or hand used in game.

Hello, But I'm Gone

Activity Level: 3   Age Level: 4+
Location: In or Outside   Group Size: 7

Game Description:

Children sit in a circle with one standing on the outside. She pats someone on the head and each runs in opposite directions around the circle. When they meet they must stop and shake hands and say **"Hello, But I'm Gone "**. The first player runs and sits down and the second proceeds around the circle and repeats the game.

Special Hints:

Great fun for the little ones.

Strike the Pose

Activity Level: 3   Age Level: 6+
Location: In or Outside   Group Size: 8

Game Description:

Two leave the room. Rest of group decides on a pose that is specific but not too detailed. The two come back in and begin striking poses. The group signals hot or cold until the two strike the group pose.

Variations:

Only one leaves the room.

Special Hints:

Vary pose complexity according to age level. Many moves should be tried at first until the group reacts.

Alternate Leaning

Activity Level: 3   Age Level: 6+

Location: In or Outside   Group Size: 20

Game Description:

Circle up with arms linked. Alternate people are **"ins"** and **"outs"**. At the signal players lean either in or out. By supporting one another a steep lean can be achieved.

Variations:

Hold hands, do it in rhythm

Special Hints:

Keep feet stationery—the more people the better.

Hold Me Up

Activity Level: 3   Age Level: 7+

Location: In or Outside   Group Size: 2

Game Description:

Partners face off then slowly fall away and catch one another by the arm—pull up close and then fall away again and catch by another part of the arm.

Variations:

One arm or two arms, try groups of threes or fours.

Special Hints:

Go slow and make sure all are comfortable.

How Many Are Standing?

Activity Level: 3   Age Level: 4+

Location: In or Outside   Group Size: 8

Game Description:

Sit in a circle. Anyone stands up whenever they want to, but cannot remain standing longer than five seconds. Aim of the game is to have exactly four standing at one time.

Variations:

Vary group size and amount standing or time up.

Special Hints:

Great for an icebreaker and for the little ones.

Feeling Sculpture

Activity Level: 3   Age Level: 8+

Location: In or Outside   Group Size: 4

Game Description:

Partner **A** whispers a feeling word into partner **B**'s ear. **B** sculpts **A** into a representation of that feeling. After one minute they find another pair. Each pair tries to guess the other's feeling. Add charades if necessary.

Variations:

Do it in groups.

Special Hints:

Don't forget to shape the face.

Still Photograph

Activity Level: 3   Age Level: 8+
Location: In or Outside   Group Size: 4

Game Description:
One player takes a few members of the group and tells them of an experience when she was happy. She then places them in a frozen picture recalling that time. The rest of the group has to guess the situation.

Variations:
Other emotions—vary group size—share tableaux with the larger group.

Special Hints:
Encourage detail. Stimulates compassion. Group children having difficulty together here.

Use That Rope

Activity Level: 3   Age Level: 3+
Location: In or Outside   Group Size: 4
Materials: rope

Game Description:
Using jump ropes children make letters—numbers—geometric shapes—flowers etc.

Variations:
Change size of rope—number of children—ways in which rope shapes interrelate.

Special Hints:
Fade into background but stay close to help maintain flow.

Find Your Animal Mate

Activity Level: 3　　　　　　　Age Level: 3+
Location: In or Outside　　　Group Size: 8

Game Description:

Animal names are written on a piece of paper. Each animal is named twice. The children are each given a slip so they know only their animal. Then they act out the animal while trying to find their partner. When two find each other they ask the elder if they are right.

Variations:

Without sounds.

Nature Acting

Activity Level: 3　　　　　　　Age Level: 3+
Location: In or Outside　　　Group Size: 4

Game Description:

A child acts out a real life situation; e.g., a butterfly drinking from a flower, or a teacher reprimanding a student, and the others try to guess what it is.

Variations:

Use props—let children act in groups.

Special Hints:

Encourage children to come up with their own ideas but be there to help. Don't let anyone make fun by putting down another.

37

Animal Acting

Activity Level: 3   Age Level: 3+
Location: In or Outside   Group Size: 5

Game Description:
Children choose an animal and act it out. Others try to guess what it is.

Variations:
Have the animal doing something, use sounds.

Special Hints:
Let the children choose their own animal, if possible.

Use That Body

Activity Level: 3   Age Level: 4+
Location: In or Outside   Group Size: 4

Game Description:
Together the children make numbers—shapes—letters—with their bodies. Everyone in the group must be included.

Special Hints:
Use small groups.

Gyrating Reptile

Activity Level: 3   Age Level: 4+

Location: In or Outside Group Size: 5

Game Description:

Children lie on the floor and grab the ankles of the child in front of them making one big snake. Then, gyrating energetically, they try to move across the floor.

Variations:

Over obstacles—against time.

Special Hints:

Ask the children for ideas.

Blind Walks

Activity Level: 3   Age Level: 6+

Location: In or Outside Group Size: 2

Materials: Blindfolds

Game Description:

In pairs—with one blindfolded—the children lead one another.

Variations:

Obstacles—in Nature.

Special Hints:

Builds self esteem to trust and be trusted. Instruct to be careful.

39

Spaghetti

Activity Level: 3   Age Level: 6+
Location: In or Outside   Group Size: 6

Game Description:

All stand in a circle. Join hands but not with the person on either side. Now untangle without letting go of hands.

Special Hints:

Sometimes it cannot be done. Give all a chance to move people around. See introduction.

Tied Together

Activity Level: 3   Age Level: 5+
Location: In or Outside   Group Size: 6

Game Description:

Two children hide their eyes. The others join hands and make themselves into the craziest knot they can. The two open their eyes and try to undo the knot without breaking hand–holds.

Variations:

Eyes closed.

Special Hints:

Make sure all get a chance to be the undoers.

Rhythm Learning

Activity Level: 3   Age Level: 6+

Location: In or Outside   Group Size: 2

Materials: Large ball

Game Description:

In pairs, children pass a ball back and forth while calling out letters of the alphabet.

Variations:

Spell words—names of animals or familiar people—do simple mathematics.

Special Hints:

Keep a rhythm going, perhaps by handclapping but do not make it too fast to exclude anyone.

Move Softly

Activity Level: 3   Age Level: 8+

Location: In or Outside   Group Size: 6

Materials: Blindfold/rag for treasure

Game Description:

One child sits on the ground guarding a treasure with the referee standing behind her. She "falls asleep"— wearing a blindfold—and the others try to creep up as quietly as possible to steal the treasure. If the child hears someone she points in that direction and everyone freezes. If the referee agrees that the miser pointed directly at the person, that person must take three steps backward.

Special Hints:

Be the referee or allow a child to be referee.

41

Blanket Toss

Activity Level: 3   Age Level: 6+
Location: In or Outside   Group Size: 6
Materials: balloons and blanket

Game Description:

Cut a hole in the blanket. Place balloons on it. Players grab edges of blanket and try to maneuver the balloon through the hole.

Variations:

Can score, with smaller values given to smaller balloons and larger values given to larger balloons.

Special Hints:

Join the fun!

Face to Face

Activity Level: 3   Age Level: 3+
Location: In or Outside   Group Size: 2

Game Description:

Partners stand a couple of feet apart. One closes her eyes and gently moves forward trying to connect noses. The other stands still.

Variations:

Both have eyes closed—introduce breathing as a clue.

Special Hints:

Good for special relationships.

In and Out

Activity Level: 3

Age Level: 5+

Location: In or Outside

Group Size: 2

Game Description:

Partners face one another with feet spread to shoulder width. With hands up, palms open, bodies rigid, the partners lean forward and catch one another. Then push off and spring back up.

Variations:

Vary distance to limit of capabilities.

Special Hints:

Play on soft surface—match pairs consciously.

Ocean Friends

Activity Level: 3

Age Level: 3+

Location: In or Outside

Group Size: ?

Materials: Beanbags

Game Description:

Fill rooms with (imaginary) water. Players swim around with beanbags on head. Dropped bag means player freezes. Friend must take deep breath, dive down and replace bag. End by pulling plug and all whirlpool closer and closer to center.

Variations:

Practice deep breath before starting, children may use one finger to hold beanbag on.

43

Pasta

Activity Level: 3

Location: Inside

Age Level: 3+

Group Size: 6

Game Description:

Players are a package of pasta, bundled close. As pot boils, players begin to relax and eventually end up in a limp pile on the floor.

Rocks in a Creek

Activity Level: 3

Location: In or Outside

Age Level: 4+

Group Size: 8

Game Description:

Players put hands on hips and slowly spin "downstream" together. As elbows touch, arms go down, simulating wearing down of sharp edges. Dizzy players crouch at bottom of creek, face upstream, extend arms back and wiggle open hands like rippling water.

Special Hints:

Talk about water as energy, transporting and rounding rocks.

Wooden Children

Activity Level: 3   Age Level: 4+
Location: Outside   Group Size: 8

Game Description:

Several players lie on backs, totally stiff being *logs*. Others cooperate to lift these *logs* and place them as corner poles for a house, or put them in a stove. Players huddle in house or warm themselves around stove.

Variations:

Other pole applications. Other players dig imaginary holes for posts. Talk about the many gifts trees give us.

Don't Let Go

Activity Level: 3   Age Level: 5+
Location: In or Outside   Group Size: 2

Game Description:

Partners face off, extend arms and hold hands. Now move into positions that would leave each partner totally off balance were it not for the support of the other.

Variations:

Support with different parts than hands. Try with more than two people.

Special Hints:

Tell each player to explore all kinds of new positions—quiet music is nice—builds trust.

Indian Ball Pass

Activity Level: 3   Age Level: 5+

Location: In or Outside   Group Size: 5

Materials: Ball

Game Description:

Players sit on floor in tight circle and extend feet towards the center. A ball is placed on one player's lap. The idea is to move the ball around the circle as fast as possible without using hands.

Variations:

Vary the size and number of balls—reverse the direction of the ball.

Special Hints:

Lots of fun—if it doesn't work the first time, try again.

Slow Motion Tag

Activity Level: 3   Age Level: 5+

Location: In or Outside   Group Size: 12

Game Description:

Slow motion tag. When tagged, a person joins "**It**". When 4 players are joined as "**It**", they split into two's and tag others. When everyone is tagged all chant "*A-moe-ba*", so all will know that the game is over.

Variations:

Vary the split size of the "**It**" group, with over–all number of players.

Special Hints:

Remember—move in slow motion.

A Chance to Be Nice

Activity Level: 3   Age Level: 3+
Location: In or Outside   Group Size: 8+

Game Description:

Players line up facing one another. Taking turns each player skips down the line while the others say something nice about that person.

Special Hints:

Make sure no sarcasm surfaces. Wait until your group begins to feel good about one another. Come back to it later if it fails the first time. An easy way to say something nice about someone else.

Inuit Ball Pass

Activity Level: 3   Age Level: 8+
Location: In or Outside   Group Size: 8
Materials: Sand filled ball or similar substitute.

Game Description:

Players kneel in a circle and pass the ball from person to person with a flat, open hand (palm up). The aim is to move the ball as rapidly as possible around the circle without actually grasping it.

Variations:

Use more than one ball at a time.

Special Hints:

Learn to play with two hands first.

Strange Positions

Activity Level: 3

Location: Inside

Age Level: 4+

Group Size: 5

Game Description:

The leader tells players to get into a strange position and hold it. The leader then tells them to get into a second strange position and so on. Positions should involve more than one player.

Special Hints:

For the very young.

Hold That Floor

Activity Level: 3

Location: Inside

Age Level: 4+

Group Size: 5

Game Description:

Players run around until leader calls "*Freeze*" and a number. Players must stop and touch the number of body parts to the floor that the leader called.

Variations:

When "*Freeze*" is called players have to find a partner and get the body parts down together.

Shoe Mates

Activity Level: 3

Age Level: 6+

Location: Inside

Group Size: 12

Game Description:

Players take off shoes and pile them in the middle. Each player selects an unmatched pair of shoes neither of which are her own. All walk around trying to find shoe mates and stand next to people so that shoes are matched in pairs.

Special Hints:

Remind big people not to crush little shoes.

Kids Carapace

Activity Level: 3

Age Level: 3+

Location: Inside

Group Size: 5

Materials: Blanket, tarp or gym mat.

Game Description:

The group gets on its hands and knees and tries to move a large shell (blanket) in one direction.

Variations:

Over an obstacle—play out turtle stories.

Special Hints:

Give them time to realize they all need to move in the same direction.

49

Whose Shoe?

Activity Level: 3

Location: Inside

Materials: Shoes

Age Level: 6+

Group Size: 5

Game Description:

Each child takes off one shoe and puts it in a pile. Everyone picks up someone else's shoe and while some-how holding it—joins hands and forms a circle. Shoe owners are identified and shoes must be returned while holding hands.

All Paint

Activity Level: 3

Location: Inside

Materials: large paper and paint

Age Level: 4+

Group Size: 6

Game Description:

A shape is drawn on a large piece of paper. The paper is hung at a height such that the tallest in the group must jump her highest to reach the top of the shape. Children dip their fingers in paint and—jumping up—try to fill the shape in.

Variations:

Use letters or numbers as shapes.

Special Hints:

Vary heights in each group making sure the shortest gets the bottom to fill. Teaches non verbal sharing.

Marble Tracking

Activity Level: 3

Age Level: 7+

Location: Outside

Group Size: 3

Materials: PVC pipe and marbles.

Game Description:

Cut 1" PVC pipe in half lengthwise. Use these tracks on a slope to make a downhill run for the marbles.

Variations:

Steep downhill, slow switchbacks, introduce obstacles.

Special Hints:

Help set it up, participate yourself, let the children make their own courses.

Hug a Tree

Activity Level: 3

Age Level: 5+

Location: Outside

Group Size: 2

Materials: Blindfold

Game Description:

In pairs, one child leads another—who is blindfolded—to a tree by a circuitous route. The blindfolded one explores the tree with all other senses and then is led back to the starting point. Blindfold removed, she sets out to find her tree.

Variations:

Hug an anything.

Special Hints:

Try to find a heavily wooded area. Talk about trees.

51

Jump Jump Jump

Activity Level: 3   Age Level: 3+
Location: Outside   Group Size: 5

Game Description:
Each child jumps in succession. The aim is to see how far the group can collectively jump.

Variations:
Over obstacles—estimate the jumps to a certain spot.

Special Hints:
Vary the order in which children jump. Encourage them to beat their old mark.

Probably Wet

Activity Level: 3   Age Level: 6+
Location: Outside   Group Size: 6
Materials: Cups and water.

Game Description:
Players stand in a circle with an empty paper cup in their teeth. One cup is filled with water and players attempt to pass the water from cup to cup without spilling it. No hands.

Variations:
Fill more cups—widen the circle.

Special Hints:
Make sure it is "OK" with each child to get wet.

Sounds and Colors

Activity Level: 3   Age Level: 6+
Location: Outside   Group Size: 4

Game Description:

In a natural setting, children lie on their backs with eyes closed. Every time one hears a new bird call they raise a finger. Then, looking around with eyes open, do the same for new colors.

Variations:

Use any sounds. See if they can count to ten without hearing a new call or seeing a new color.

Special Hints:

Emphasize quietness.

Unnature Trail

Activity Level: 3   Age Level: 6+
Location: Outside   Group Size: 6

Materials: Various unnatural objects such as paper clips or bobby pins.

Game Description:

Along a trail, hide a dozen human made objects. Some should be easy to find, others well hidden. The children try to find them, but do not touch them. They report their findings to the teacher who sends them back to look for any they have missed.

Special Hints:

Hide a paper bag well. It is unlikely it will be found and will facilitate a discussion about camouflage which is one of the aims of this activity.

Duplicate

Activity Level: 3

Location: Outside

Age Level: 8+

Group Size: 4

Materials: Naturally found objects and a cloth

Game Description:

Collect several naturally occurring objects from the game area. Place them on the ground, covered by the cloth. Lifting the cloth for 30 seconds let the children study the objects then cover again. Then tell them to go find objects like them in the area.

Variations:

Vary time to study—number of objects.

Special Hints:

Pull objects out one at a time to see who has the match. Careful not to let this game get competitive.

Tree Silhouettes

Activity Level: 3

Location: Outside

Age Level: 6+

Group Size: 5

Game Description:

In a place where several different tree types grow, have a child shape herself like a tree. The others try to guess which tree she is imitating.

Variations:

Use groups—do any natural formation.

Special Hints:

Can be worked in with real life drama.

Handle With Care

Activity Level: 3
Location: Outside
Materials: Big Leaves

Age Level: 4+
Group Size: 5

Game Description:

Players stand in line. A broad leaf is passed overhead until it reaches the back of the line. Then that person brings it to the front and starts again. The aim is for everyone to be first and not to damage the leaf.

Variations:

Do it with any natural object.

Special Hints:

Talk about leaves—damage humans due to nature—ecology.

Path Finder

Activity Level: 3
Location: Outside

Age Level: 5+
Group Size: 6

Game Description:

Divide players into two groups. Each group marks their own nature trail using only natural objects. Dots of flour are "OK" but do not deface anything. Meet back at starting place and then each group follows the other's trail.

Variations:

Vary the terrain—including through water.

Special Hints:

Don't let one group make it too hard for the other until the game has been played a few times—builds children's confidence in natural settings.

Prooie

Activity Level: 3

Age Level: 7+

Location: In or Out

Group Size: 10

Game Description:

Players scatter around a defined area. All close their eyes. Leader moves through group and silently chooses one player to be "Prooie". Prooie opens her eyes. Leader gives signal to begin. All except Prooie start wandering around, keeping their eyes closed. As they bump into each other, they say "Prooie"? If the person answers "Prooie" they separate and continue to wander. The object is to find the Prooie, who never answers back. When they bump into Prooie, ask their question and receive no reply, they open their eyes and join hands with Prooie. Game continues until all are joined as Prooie.

Special Hints:

Make sure all keep eyes closed. If games ends too quickly, expand boundaries.

Indian Chief *(page 63) — leader should make the movements very graphic without being too tiring for little ones.*

Guess Our Shape *(page 70) — towards peace with cooperative games.*

Are We Near You?

Activity Level: 4   Age Level: 7+

Location: Outside   Group Size: 6

Materials: Blindfold

Game Description:

Best played on a narrow hiking trail. One child sent ahead on the trail until she is out of sight. She steps off the trail and sits, blindfolded. After she is settled, the leader starts the group walking. They walk slowly, carefully and as silently as possible. **No Talking**. The object of the game is for the group to secretly file past the blindfolded player. When the blindfolded one thinks she hears them she points and says aloud "I hear you" When she guesses, another child takes her turn.

Variations:

Have the blindfolded child cup her hands behind her ears to amplify the sound—Group can file past one by one, or as a unit.

Special Hints:

The blindfolded child can be the prey; a deer, mouse, etc. The group are predators; coyote, hawk, humans, etc. Discuss both roles afterwards. Often the prey has feelings of being hunted. Group frustrations often surface if one or two make a noise which reveals the whole group.

Rhythm Pulse

Activity Level: 4   Age Level: 6+
Location: In or Out   Group Size: 4

Game Description:

Group sits in a circle with hands joined. One person starts a pattern of squeezes in one direction. This pattern is a pulse. For example: 3 quick squeezes, followed by two long squeezes. The pulse is passed around the circle until it is back with the person who started it. Object is to keep the pulse from altering.

Special Hints:

No more than 8 people so everyone has a chance to start a pulse before tiring of the game—Excellent for quieting and focusing energy—good at the end of the day—If played with less than five, use complicated pulses—Short discussion of each pulse interesting.

Sleeper

Activity Level: 4   Age Level: 7+
Location: In or Out   Group Size: 10

Game Description:

Players cover eyes. Leader silently chooses Sleeper. Players open eyes and start to mingle. Sleeper puts a player to sleep by winking once at her. Player counts silently to 3 and falls asleep on the floor. Play continues until someone guesses who the Sleeper is.

Variations:

Can be played sitting in a circle.

Special Hints:

Encourage players to look into each other's eyes—No guessing who Sleeper is until one person is asleep—Encourage players to be discreet with their winks. One guess per player as to who sleeper is.

Find Your Rock

Activity Level: 4   Age Level: 4+
Location: Out   Group Size: 6
Materials: A cloth to lay rocks on

Game Description:

Each player finds a special rock. Give them 4 minutes to get to know it using all senses. Place rocks on cloth or cleared surface. Group sits around rock pile. With their eyes closed they try to find their rock by touch. When they believe they have theirs, they open their eyes to see if they are right.

Variations:

Place large cloth over rocks so they can search with eyes open—add rocks that belong to nobody—use other natural objects.

Special Hints:

At first make suggestions as they feel their rocks; warm?, smooth? —Establish size limits so they are encouraged to notice characteristics other than size.

Canyon Echo

Activity Level: 4

Location: Out

Age Level: 5+

Group Size: 4

Game Description:

Group is on a trail, single file. First and last in line are the canyon walls. All the players in between are the canyon air that the echo travels through. The head of the line, person 1, starts the echo. Echo can be any sound or noise pattern. The echo is passed from person to person down the canyon air until it hits the canyon wall, which is the last person in the line. The wall then starts a new and different echo which travels through the air to person 1 again. After voicing the echo, person 1 steps off the trail and rejoins the line after it files past, becoming the end of the line, or the opposite canyon wall. The new lead person starts a new echo.

Variations:

Introduce a movement to go with sound.

Special Hints:

Encourage many different sounds—Start game with story about canyons and echos—Great for children who are getting tired or bored while hiking for they begin to focus on one another rather than discomfort—Keeps children from getting separated from group.

In Between

Activity Level: 4   Age Level: 3+

Location: In or Outside   Group Size: 2

Materials: large rubber ball or other objects depending upon variations.

Game Description:

Two children face one another and balance a ball between their bodies without using hands.

Variations:

Increase amount of players—substitute other objects for the ball—have players hold a board and balance objects on the board—let them walk around.

Special Hints:

Increase complexity to keep it interesting—help the little ones—do it yourself.

Two Way Copy

Activity Level: 4   Age Level: 4+

Location: In or Outside   Group Size: 2

Game Description:

First, two children face one another. One moves and the others mirrors her movements. Next, one child stands behind the other. As the first one moves, the following child shadows the movements.

Variations:

Limit to the face—allow movement in Mirrors.

Special Hints:

Good for mixed ages—older children will enjoy doing this with little ones—do not let it become competitive—vary the partners.

Pinocchio

Activity Level: 4 Age Level: 4+

Location: In or Outside Group Size: 2

Game Description:

One partner is puppet on the ground unable to move. The other child is puppeteer and moves the child by pulling imaginary strings.

Special Hints:

Do a few practice turns so children get the feel—vary partners—subtle non–verbal communication skills enhanced.

Talking Without Words

Activity Level: 4 Age Level: 4+

Location: In or Outside Group Size: 2

Game Description:

One player makes nonsense sounds and the partner responds with a movement showing how the sound made her feel. A conversation develops.

Variations:

Do it in larger groups—Bring in props.

Special Hints:

Start with short interactions and let "vocabularies" build in time—new dimension in communication.

Clothes Switch

Activity Level: 4   Age Level: 5+
Location: In or Outside   Group Size: 2
Materials: Large old shirt

Game Description:

One player wears a very large old shirt. Partners hold hands. The aim is to get the shirt onto the second partner without letting go of the hands.

Special Hints:

Help the little ones. Let older ones having conflict try this one together.

Indian Chief

Activity Level: 4   Age Level: 4+
Location: In or Outside   Group Size: 8

Game Description:

One player goes where she cannot see the others. A leader is chosen. She does a movement which the others follow. The leader changes movement regularly. The others follow the leader's movement. The hidden one returns and by watching everyone tries to guess who the leader is.

Variations:

Send more than one away and have them confer— limit the guesses. Have two leaders and switch off movements. Use movements that make no sound.

Special Hints:

Join the fun!

Hit the Nail

Activity Level: 4   Age Level: 4+

Location: In or Outside   Group Size: 4

Materials: Board, hammer and nails.

Game Description:

Start a nail in a board. Now each player takes one turn hitting the nail. See how few strokes the class can use to get the nail all the way in.

Variations:

Use the weaker arm—blindfolded—vary nail size or hammer size. Apply the same principle to sawing through wood.

Special Hints:

Watch out for "machos." Make sure no one gets hurt.

I Am

Activity Level: 4   Age Level: 5+

Location: In or Outside   Group Size: 7

Game Description:

All stand in a circle. Taking turns each player goes to the middle calls her name and makes a sound and movement. Then everyone imitates the person in the middle while she watches. Then the next person goes.

Variations:

If the group is close have one child do another's name. Be an animal instead of yourself.

Special Hints:

Good for warm–up or introductions. Good for group recentering.

Psychic Nonsense

Activity Level: 4

Location: In or Outside

Age Level: 5+

Group Size: 2

Game Description:

Players decide on three sound and motion movements. One example of a sound and motion movement is flapping the arms and cawing as a crow. They then turn their backs to one another. On the count of three, they turn around and do one of the three movements. The aim is for everyone to do the same one.

Special Hints:

Join the fun!

A What?

Activity Level: 4

Location: In or Outside

Materials: Two balls

Age Level: 7+

Group Size: 8

Game Description:

Players circle. Player **1** hands a ball to **2** and says: *"This is a banana."* "A What?", asks **2**. *"A banana"*, says **1**. *"Oh, a banana."* says **2**. **2** hands the ball to **3** and says; *"This is a banana."* *"A What?"* asks **3** to **2**. *"A What?"* asks **2** to **1**. *"A banana"* says **1** to **2**. *"A banana"*, says **2** to **3**. *"Oh, a banana."* says **3** and then turns to hand it to **4**. While the '*banana*' goes around the circle clockwise, the other ball, a '*pineapple*' goes around the circle counterclockwise, with the same verbal procedures.

Special Hints:

Practice a few times before judging this one. It always turns out to be great fun and a tension breaker. People will play it often to get it right for it is hard to make both balls go all the way around. Make up silly names for the objects (balls).

Make Me Into You

Activity Level: 4

Location: In or Outside

Age Level: 6+

Group Size: 3

Game Description:

One player closes eyes. Another forms a sculptured pose. The one with eyes closed sculpts the third player into the pose chosen by player two based on the sense of touch.

Special Hints:

No one has ever abused this game. Brings out the gentleness in people.

Subtle Pressure

Activity Level: 4

Location: In or Outside

Age Level: 9+

Group Size: 2

Game Description:

Partners face off. One puts hand on two's head and slowly presses down. Two reacts to the pressures by sinking a bit. Then slowly one's hand is lighter and two feels herself pulled up. Do it a few times and switch roles.

Special Hints:

This is a subtle and sensitive game best done with people who are caring for one another or who might be caring if given the chance.

Cast Your Vote

Activity Level: 4   Age Level: 5+
Location: In or Outside   Group Size: 6

Game Description:

Draw a line on the ground that represents a continuum from "*strongly agree*" to "*strongly disagree*". Introduce topics and let the children vote by where they stand. No talking.

Variations:

Use raising of hands or voice vote.

Special Hints:

Do not vote yourself—make jokes—include issues from classroom and family. Great for values clarification as it allows older children to express opinions on sensitive issues.

What Animal Am I?

Activity Level: 4   Age Level: 6+
Location: In or Outside   Group Size: 5
Materials: Pictures of animals and safety pins.

Game Description:

A picture of a different animal is pinned to each player's back. The player asks *yes* or *no* questions of the other players and tries to guess her animal.

Variations:

Substitute environments, buildings or people for animals.

Special Hints:

Start easy and make sure players circulate while asking questions.

Back To Back

Activity Level: 4   Age Level: 4+
Location: In or Outside   Group Size: 2

Game Description:
Two children sit back to back and attempt to get up without using their hands.

Variations:
Vary group size.

Special Hints:
If difficult, suggest they link elbows. Let children in conflict try this together.

Catch Me

Activity Level: 4   Age Level: 7+
Location: In or Outside   Group Size: 7

Game Description:
About seven children form a tight circle. One child in the middle stiffens her body and falls in any direction. The others catch her and gently push her around.

Variations:
Vary the rhythm of the passing.

Special Hints:
Make sure the children are attentive. Nice way to start the day.

Body Ball

Activity Level: 4

Location: In or Outside

Materials: Beach ball

Age Level: 4+

Group Size: 2

Game Description:
Without using hands, partners try to get a beach ball from the ground to their heads.

Variations:
Other size balls—more players.

Special Hints:
A good way to let children who are having difficulty with one another be together.

Where Is It?

Activity Level: 4

Location: In or Outside

Materials: pebble

Age Level: 6+

Group Size: 7

Game Description:
In a circle, with one player in the middle whose eyes are closed. Others pass the pebble. The one in the middle opens eyes and tries to guess who has the stone. Others keep passing it or pretend they are passing it. The pebble must always be in motion. Passes and fakes go on in both directions but always between persons next to one another.

Special Hints:
Encourage good fakery.

Circuits

Activity Level: 4   Age Level: 8+
Location: In or Outside   Group Size: 8

Game Description:

All players in a circle. Pass hand squeezes to the left saying "*laa*". Pass hand squeezes to the right saying "*maa*".

Variations:

Add and subtract movements and sounds according to abilities.

Special Hints:

A subtle game of coordination—can evolve with the children.

Guess Our Shape

Activity Level: 4   Age Level: 4+
Location: In or Outside   Group Size: 4

Game Description:

Children divide into two groups. One group decides on a shape to imitate, such as a crocodile or an ice cream cone, using every person in the group. The other group must guess what it is or get close. Then it is the other groups turn.

Special Hints:

Creates a peaceful atmosphere.

Hello

Activity Level: 4   Age Level: 3+
Location: In or Outside   Group Size: 12

Game Description:
Players in a circle. Each person attempts to make eye contact with another. Once contact is established those players change places.

Variations:
Add greetings—funny things to do or say during switching—add music—hand clapping of syllables in name as it is spoken.

Special Hints:
Excellent icebreaker—make sure everyone included.

Direct Me

Activity Level: 4   Age Level: 3+
Location: In or Outside   Group Size: 4
Materials: Rock and blindfold.

Game Description:
Children in a circle, one in the middle, blindfolded. Rock on floor. Circle tries to direct blindfolded one to step on rock.

Variations:
Vary sophistication of directions allowed—blindfold partners.

Special Hints:
Good way to teach directions to young children.

Alphabet

Activity Level: 4   Age Level: 7+
Location: In or Outside   Group Size: 10

Game Description:
Each player takes one or more letters of the alphabet; then they have to form words.

Variations:
Time the children—name a theme—make a sentence.

Special Hints:
Good for teaching spelling, etc. Can be combined with animal games.

Huh?

Activity Level: 4   Age Level: 5+
Location: Inside   Group Size: 2

Game Description:
Partners talk together without using words. They have to make up sounds that make no sense to them and carry on a conversation.

Variations:
Make the sounds in rhythm to do group poetry. Act out a theme—do movement to the sounds—have some children guess what the others are doing.

Special Hints:
One of the best for teaching communication.

72

Getting Together

Activity Level: 4

Age Level: 5+

Location: Inside

Group Size: 15

Game Description:

Count off by *one's*, *two's* and *three's*. Everyone walks around shaking hands with whomever they meet. *Ones* shake once, *twos* give two shakes and so on. When they find someone with same number they hold hands until all of the number are joined.

Special Hints:

A good way to form teams.

Chalkboard Drawing

Activity Level: 4

Age Level: 4+

Location: Inside

Group Size: 1

Materials: Chalk and chalkboard.

Game Description:

Children draw circles on chalkboard under various handicaps, i.e., in opposite direction with each hand, blindfolded, or with objects on the back of the hand.

Variations:

Change shapes—change drawing tool, i.e., chalk held in a clothespin—work a theme.

Special Hints:

Keep the focus on well drawn shapes—helps individual recentering.

Feel and Find Boxes

Activity Level: 4   Age Level: 5+
Location: Inside   Group Size: 1
Materials: Anything and everything.

Game Description:

A box is constructed with a curtain on the front. Various objects are placed in it which the children try to guess by touch.

Variations:

Change box size—objects—place duplicates on top for matching—use objects from nature.

Special Hints:

Increase complexity continually.

Human Puzzles

Activity Level: 4   Age Level: 4+
Location: Inside   Group Size: 5
Materials: Home made puzzle pieces.

Game Description:

In groups of 5 to 7, each child is given a piece of a puzzle. Working together they put their puzzle together.

Variations:

Increase complexity. Let group puzzles fit together to make one large puzzle. Let each group make up a story about their puzzle. Let each story be a chapter in the class story puzzle.

Silent Drawing *(page 79) — a partner game for quiet sharing among all ages.*

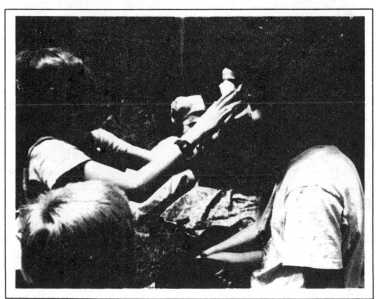

Do You Know Me? *(page 84) — getting in touch with your friends.*

Mime Rhyme

Activity Level: 4

Age Level: 8+

Location: Inside

Group Size: 4+

Game Description:

Person thinks up word and tells others a word that rhymes with it. Others try to guess word but must act out their guess in pantomime. Person tells whether that guess is right.

Special Hints:

Good for new groups—rainy days—improving communication.

Watch My Face

Activity Level: 5

Age Level: 4+

Location: In or Outside

Group Size: 8

Game Description:

Players in a circle. One player starts a crazy face one way. When that one is going she starts another one going the other way. When it makes the round someone else begins.

Variations:

Add a sound.

What Did I Do?

Activity Level: 5   Age Level: 6+
Location: In or Outside   Group Size: 2

Game Description:
Partners face off. **A** examines **B** for a minute or two and then turns her back. **B** changes five things about her appearance. **A** turns around and tries to guess what has been changed.

Variations:
Vary the time of observation—amount of things changed. Do it with an area and not a person.

Special Hints:
Help out those who get stumped. Don't let it become competitive.

Webs

Activity Level: 5   Age Level: 5+
Location: In or Outside   Group Size: 5
Materials: Ball of yarn.

Game Description:
Using a big ball of yarn hold the end and toss the rest to another. All are seated in a circle. The person with the yarn gets to speak to the group. The ball is passed, the end is held, the web is formed.

Variations:
Introduce a theme on which all have to speak.

Special Hints:
Allow the option to pass without speaking. Play fairly regularly for group solidarity. Let important issues arise.

Try Not To Laugh

Activity Level: 5   Age Level: 4+

Location: In or Outside   Group Size: 4

Game Description:

Players sit in a circle. One is **It** and calls "*Muk*". This ends all conversation and smiling. It is now up to the one who is **It** to make another talk or smile. Anything goes but no touching and no averting eyes.

Special Hints:

Play along—introduce surprise. A good way to calm things down.

ReConnect

Activity Level: 5   Age Level: 5+

Location: In or Outside   Group Size: 2

Game Description:

Eyes closed, partners face off, touch palms, feel the energy and drop arms. Then take two steps back, turn 3 times and try to reconnect palms.

Variations:

Bend arms and try to touch agreed upon other body part—do it in a circle.

Special Hints:

It's fun to watch, so make it a group activity even if only two are playing.

Nature Web

Activity Level: 5

Location: In or Outside

Materials: Ball of yarn.

Age Level: 8+

Group Size: 5

Game Description:

Holding a ball of yarn the leader asks the first child to name a plant. The ball of yarn is thrown to number **1**. Then ask: "*What animal eats that plant?*" The ball is thrown to the second respondant, **2**, with **1** holding the end. Then ask:"*What animal eats that animal?*" The yarn is thrown to **3**. Then: "*Where does that animal live?*" And so on until a web representing the local ecology is formed. Then introduce a plausible disaster. Tug on the point of the web that represented that part of the environment that would be destroyed. Who else feels the tug? And so on.

Special Hints:

Here's safe space for everyone to communicate their values concerning the environment.

Silent Structures

Activity Level: 5

Age Level: 6+

Location: Inside

Group Size: 4

Materials: Colored paper, masking tape, scissors.

Game Description:
Divide children into groups of 4 to 6. Give each group two scissors, two rolls of masking tape and a stack of colored paper. One color per group. Tell the children to build a castle. No talking allowed.

Variations:
Allow talking—using random materials at hand.

Special Hints:
Hold a discussion afterwards to bring out decision making role of each child. Vary group make-up. Builds non verbal communication skills.

Silent Drawing

Activity Level: 5

Age Level: 4+

Location: Inside

Group Size: 2

Materials: Drawing tools, painting tools, and large sheets of paper.

Game Description:
Two players hold the same brush or crayon and draw on the same piece of paper. No talking.

Variations:
Have several pairs draw on the same piece of paper. Let one pair finish before the next begins—suggest a theme.

Special Hints:
Vary partners—encourage slow starters.

Where Did It Go?

Activity Level: 5
Location: Inside
Materials: Small bell.

Age Level: 5+
Group Size: 6

Game Description:

One player sits in the middle blindfolded. The other players pass a bell around with each player ringing it once. They stop and the last one puts it behind her back. The one in the center tries to guess where it is.

Dictionary

Activity Level: 5
Location: Inside
Materials: Dictionary, pencils and papers.

Age Level: 10
Group Size: 5

Game Description:

One player picks a strange word from the dictionary. She writes it down on a slip of paper. She says the word. Everyone else writes down their definition of the word. Then the definitions are read aloud and everyone tries to guess which one was right.

Variations:

Try to guess who wrote which definition.

Special Hints:

Great for vocabulary building. Can be great fun for elders.

T-Shirts

Activity Level: 5

Age Level: 4+

Location: Inside

Group Size: 6

Materials: T-shirt outline on a piece of paper and drawing implements

Game Description:

Give each child a piece of paper with a T-shirt outlined on it. Let them cut the shirt out and write their name in the middle. Then ask them questions about their life and values and have them write or draw the answers on various parts of the shirt.

Variations:

Examples: favorite animal, place in home or memory.

Special Hints:

Allow time for decorating—excellent for insight into values—builds self esteem.

Collage

Activity Level: 5

Age Level: 5+

Location: Inside

Group Size: 4

Materials: Glue, scissors, old magazines and poster board.

Game Description:

A theme is introduced and the group collectively creates a collage.

Variations:

Any theme—can make a group gift.

Special Hints:

Good for a rainy day.

Prehistoric Communication

Activity Level: 5   Age Level: 8+

Location: Inside   Group Size: 4

Materials: Paper and drawing utensil.

Game Description:

Form groups of 4. One from each group comes to the leader who whispers a word in her ear. That person returns to the group and draws the word or phrase while the others try to guess. Then another player gets a new word.

Variations:

Two do the drawing holding one drawing tool either communicating with one another or not. Can draw more than one picture.

Special Hints:

If it goes too long, the next person goes.

Guess

Activity Level: 5   Age Level: 4+

Location: Inside   Group Size: 5+

Materials: Weird hand held objects and sheet.

Game Description:

Players sit in a circle with sheet covering hands and lower arms. Weird object passed around under the sheet and everyone tries to guess what it is.

Variations:

Choose object suitable to level of players.

Special Hints:

Let little ones feel first before guessing. Guess in turn and don't reveal until end—or guess silently so no one feels left out.

Co-op Story Telling

Activity Level: 5
Location: In or Outside

Age Level: 3+
Group Size: 3

Game Description:
Players make up a story one sentence at a time, with each player taking a turn.

Variations:
Each player takes a paragraph—introduce a theme— elder takes the lead and keeps the theme alive.

Special Hints:
Encourage all to play—excellent around campfire— can lead to collective picture.

Lion, Fox, Deer, Dove

Activity Level: 5
Location: Inside

Age Level: 7+
Group Size: 12

Materials: Four pieces of poster board; marker.

Game Description:
Make a poster board sign for *Lion, Fox, Deer* and *Dove*. Ask the players to go the animal that they most resemble when they join a new group. Let them discuss amongst themselves why they picked that animal. Then a spokesperson from each group explains to everyone the feelings and thoughts of her animal group.

Variations:
Pick other animals—other issues to discuss.

Special Hints:
The discussion is critical. It will reveal the predispositions of the players.

Cooperative House Play

Activity Level: 5

Age Level: 3+

Location: In or Outside

Group Size: 2

Materials: Varies with house play engaged.

Game Description:

Work around the house can be turned into a cooperative adventure. Cooking can be done with only one hand, or with only one person knowing the recipe and no talking allowed. Gardening can also be done under similar handicaps to promote cooperation.

Variations:

Limited only by your imagination.

Special Hints:

Approach with good humor and no time limit.

Do You Know Me?

Activity Level: 5

Age Level: 4+

Location: In or Out

Group Size: 8

Materials: Blindfold

Game Description:

A blindfolded player is led to the group sitting in a line or semicircle. She is told to identify one person in the group by gently touching everyone's face, one by one, until she finds who she is looking for. After she guesses, the blindfold is removed and another goes.

Variations:

Identification by touching hands only—Identify each person as they are touched.

Special Hints:

Only touch face, not clothing or jewelry—**silence is critical**

Casual Conversation

Activity Level: 5   Age Level: 8+

Location: In or Out   Group Size: 6

Game Description:

Group sends 2 people out of earshot then decides on two different sentences. The pair is called back and each is privately told one of the sentences. The pair proceed to have a "conversation". Each tries to insert their sentence into the conversation before the other. If the other speaker suspects the sentence has been said, she can challenge. Each player is allowed three challenges. When the sentence is either challenged correctly or passes undetected the game is over and two new players go.

Special Hints:

Younger children will need some coaching at first—Remind them to develop conversation before attempting to insert sentence. Sample sentences: *"When salmon spawn they turn bright red." "Human beings have 40 million brain cells."* Good game to pair children who don't often talk to each other or play together. With care, it serves to pair children who don't get along.

Books About Cooperative Games

Cornell, Joseph Bharat. *Sharing Nature with Children.* Nevada City, CA: Ananda Publications, 1979. $7.95 Learn about nature while playing. Great, imaginative fun.

Deacove, Jim. *Sports Manual of Non-Competitive Games and Games Manual of Non-Competitve Games.* Family Pastimes, R.R. 4, Perth, Ont. K7h3C6. Two excellent, innovative booklets that include both original ideas and modifications on competitive events. A pioneer in the field.

Flugelman, Andrew, ed. *The New Games Book* and *The Second New Games Book.* New York, NY: 1977 $7.95 Generally vibrant, but some competitive games.

Gibbs, J. and Allen A. *Tribes.* Berkeley, CA: Center Source Publications, 1978. $10.00 Compendium of self esteem building activities. Designed for teachers, but useful for everyone.

Harrison, Marta. *For the Fun Of It; Selected Cooperative Games.* A peace activists selection of games. Philadelphia, PA: New Society Publishers, 1976. $9.95 Description of the relationship between play and non-violence.

Orlick, Terry. *The Cooperative Sports and Games Book.* New York, NY: Pantheon, 1978. $8.95; and The Second Cooperative Sports and Games Book. Also Pantheon. $9.95. Many games, including those from other cultures. Exposition of the philosophy of Cooperative Games and Activities.

Rohnke, Karl. *Silver Bullets: A Guide to Initiative Problems, Adventure Games, Stunts and Trust Activities.*

Sobel, Jeffrey. *Everybody Wins*. Walker Publications, 1984. $8.95. Many games, well presented, valuable for all ages, especially the younger ones.

Weinstein, Max, and Goodman, M. *PlayFair*. San Luis Obispo, CA: Impact Publishers, 1980. $9.95 Exuberant account of many unique games and the way to introduce and play them.

You, the reader. *The Game YOU Invent.* Your home. Free! These are the the best games of all!

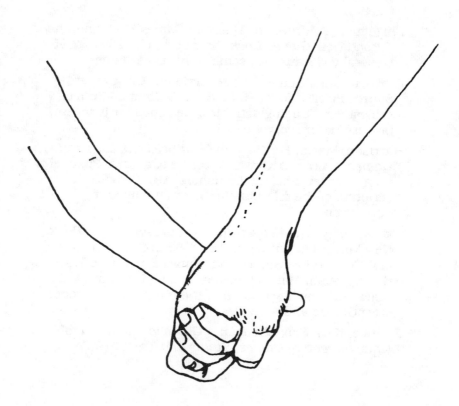

Games Group Size Guide

One or More Players

Two or More Players

Three or More Players

Four or More Players

Five or More Players

Six or More Players

Seven or More Players

Eight or More Players

Games Age Level Guide

Age Five and Up

Age Six and Up

Age Seven and Up

Age Eight and Up

Age Nine and Up

Notes

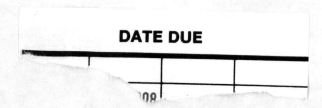

DATE DUE